An Unauthorized Biography By Lexi Ryals

MIRANDA MANIA

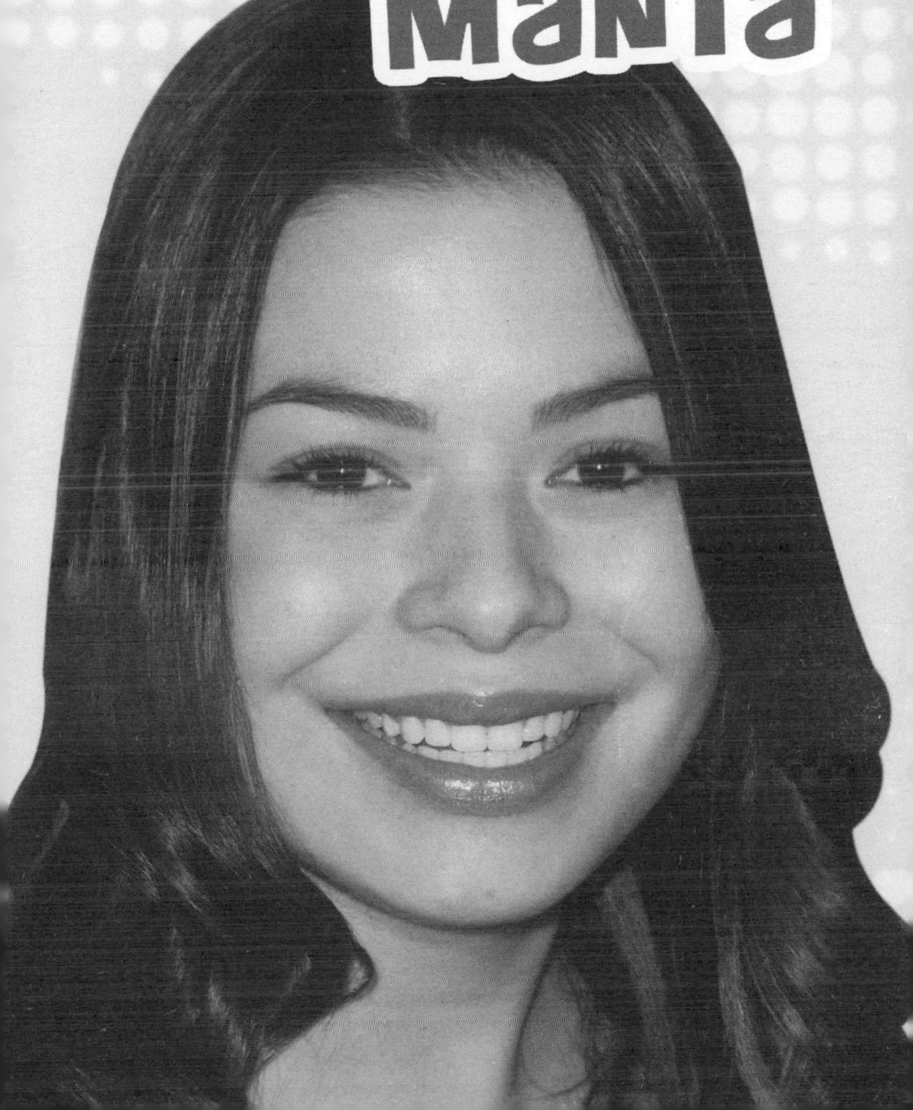

PRICE STERN SLOAN
Published by the Penguin Group
Penguin Group (USA) Inc., 375 Hudson Street, New York, New York 10014, USA
Penguin Group (Canada), 90 Eglinton Avenue East, Suite 700,
Toronto, Ontario M4P 2Y3, Canada
(a division of Pearson Penguin Canada Inc.)
Penguin Books Ltd., 80 Strand, London WC2R 0RL, England
Penguin Group Ireland, 25 St. Stephen's Green, Dublin 2, Ireland
(a division of Penguin Books Ltd.)
Penguin Group (Australia), 250 Camberwell Road, Camberwell, Victoria 3124, Australia
(a division of Pearson Australia Group Pty. Ltd.)
Penguin Books India Pvt. Ltd., 11 Community Centre, Panchsheel Park,
New Delhi—110 017, India
Penguin Group (NZ), 67 Apollo Drive, Rosedale, North Shore 0632, New Zealand
(a division of Pearson New Zealand Ltd.)
Penguin Books (South Africa) (Pty.) Ltd., 24 Sturdee Avenue,
Rosebank, Johannesburg 2196, South Africa

Penguin Books Ltd., Registered Offices:
80 Strand, London WC2R 0RL, England

Photo credits: Cover: courtesy of © Glenn Harris/PR Photos; Insert photos:
first page courtesy of © Chris Hatcher/PR Photos; second page courtesy of Albert L. Ortega/
WireImage, Photo by Donald Weber/Getty Images; third page courtesy of Mike Guastella/
WireImage, Jason Merritt/Film Magic; fourth page courtesy of George Napolitano/FilmMagic,
Scott Gries/Getty Images for Nickelodeon.

Library of Congress Control Number: 2008017791

ISBN 978-0-8431-3368-4   10 9 8 7 6 5 4 3 2 1

An Unauthorized Biography By Lexi Ryals

MiRaNDa
MaNia

PSS!
PRICE STERN SLOAN

Table of Contents

Introduction

It was the evening before filming was scheduled to start for a brand-new pilot for Nickelodeon. The Nick Studios on Sunset Boulevard in Los Angeles, California, was buzzing as the cast and crew prepared to do one final run-through before calling it a night. It was the last time they would have the chance to practice the episode from beginning to end before filming it the next day in front of a live audience, and everyone was a little on edge hoping to get it just right. Miranda Cosgrove, the show's star, and her fellow actors were going through their blocking with the director, making sure they knew exactly where to stand in each scene. The assistant director was shouting out directions to the lighting crew, the parents and guests of the cast were waiting patiently, and a full contingent of Nickelodeon executives were speaking in hushed tones in the corner. Finally, everyone and everything was in place and the director yelled action.

Miranda transformed as soon as the lights went on. Before filming began, she was a normal laid-back teenager, but once the cameras were on she positively lit up the set. Her timing was impeccable and she delivered joke after joke as smoothly as any of the adult actors on set. Dan Schneider, the show's creator and writer, was front and center watching the performance, and his laugh rang out loud and clear at every single joke. Miranda could tell it was going well, and she was enjoying sinking deeper into her character. She knew she would be ready for the next day's filming, and she was becoming more and more confident with every scene— that is, until they came to Scene R.

In Scene R, Miranda's character and her best friend were auditioning weird acts for their new web show. The acts were made up of child actors with unusual talents, and included a rapping contortionist, a girl who hopped on a pogo stick and played the trumpet at the same time, and a boy who could supposedly inhale milk through his nose and make it come out of his eyes. Only Dan Schneider had actually seen milk come out of the boy's eyes. It was a difficult trick, which is why they had been saving it for the final rehearsal. Miranda and the rest of the cast had never even met the milk boy, and they were all curious to see what would happen when it was finally his turn to perform. When it was time for his appearance, the boy poured some milk into his cupped palm and inhaled it through his nose. Then he pinched his nostrils shut with one hand and pulled the skin down under his eyes with the other. Immediately a stream of milk shot out from under the boy's eyes and flew six feet through the air.

After a moment of stunned silence, chaos erupted on set. Miranda and the rest of the actors screamed, completely grossed out and awed by the spectacle, and the audience erupted with mixed reactions. The run-through was supposed to go on in real time to make sure the show wasn't too long or too short, but it took a while before everyone calmed down enough to proceed with the scene. After the run-through was finished, Miranda stood off to the side and shook her head in amazement as she watched the flurry of assistants cleaning up the milk from the stage. She had loved every minute of the rehearsal, but it had been an incredibly crazy day and she was ready to go home to bed. Little did Miranda know that it was just the first of many, many crazy days to come. The pilot they had been filming was for a show called *iCarly* and Miranda was playing the title character, Carly Shay. Miranda had high hopes that the show would do well, but she probably never dreamed that it would become the most popular show on Nickelodeon and change her entire life.

Chapter 1

Meet Miranda

It was a usual bright sunny day in Los Angeles, California, on May 14, 1993. But that day was anything but usual for Bill and Chris Cosgrove. The couple had just welcomed their first child into the world, a baby girl they named Miranda Taylor Cosgrove. Little Miranda would turn out to be the light of their lives and the only child they would have. With a head full of dark hair and huge brown eyes, baby Miranda was undeniably adorable and her parents were practically bursting with pride when they drove her home to Downey, California, just twenty minutes southeast of Los Angeles.

Downey is a small suburb south of L.A. and north of Long Beach. Its prime location in between these two urban areas means that Downey's major downtown intersection is one of the busiest in the United States. With all of those people driving through town, Downey's biggest claim to fame is that it is one of the fast-food capitals of the world. The oldest surviving McDonald's was built there in 1953, and it still has its original "golden arches" lit up in neon. Downey is also the home of the very first Taco Bell restaurant, opened in 1962 by Glen Bell. In addition to its historic fast food spots, Downey is known as the home of many stars. The brother and sister pop music act the Carpenters moved to Downey in 1963; hilarious comic "Weird Al" Yankovic was born in Downey; James Hetfield of Metallica graduated from Downey High School; and New York Rangers hockey star Ryan Hollweg and three-time world champion Grand Prix motorcycle racer Wayne Rainey both grew up in Downey. Living near all of that star power must have rubbed off on Miranda early on, since she now ranks up there with the rest of Downey's biggest homegrown celebrities!

The best part about growing up in Downey for

Miranda was that she got to live a small-town lifestyle, but she was still close to a big city. She spent a lot of time swimming in the ocean at some of California's gorgeous beaches and hiking in the nearby hills. She played on the playgrounds in Downey's lush, green parks with her friends, went out to breakfast with her parents on the weekends, and goofed off at the local swimming pool in the summers. But Miranda also had access to all of the cultural opportunities of Los Angeles, like live theater, concerts, and, of course, historic landmarks such as Grauman's Chinese Theatre and the Kodak Theatre. There is always something new and exciting going on in Hollywood, so, growing up, Miranda got to experience some pretty cool events nearby. The Cosgroves would often go into Los Angeles for an event or dinner out at a fancy restaurant, but they spent most of their time hanging out together in Downey. Even so, with Hollywood practically in her backyard, Miranda couldn't escape the influences of the film industry forever. In fact, as soon as Miranda could walk, her parents would find her singing and dancing in front of her bedroom mirror. As an only child, Miranda learned to keep herself entertained. Miranda made lots of friends in her neighborhood, so she didn't mind her lack of siblings. Plus, Miranda has always been extremely close to her mother. The two spend a lot of time together. They have lots of inside jokes and are always laughing over something silly that one or the other of them has done. "My mom is really funny. Maybe I get it [comedic timing] from her?!" Miranda explained to online magazine *Starry Constellation* about her famous sense of humor. That comedic timing made Miranda popular with her friends, since she could always be counted on to keep everyone laughing.

When Miranda was five years old, she started elementary school at Maude Price Elementary in Downey. She was shy at first, but she soon warmed up to the other kids in her classes and made some great friends that she is still close to today. Miranda wasn't the class clown or the teacher's pet, but she was popular, easy to get along with, and fun to be around. She considered herself a dork back then, but she was probably pretty much the same easygoing, goofy, funny girl she is today. Miranda enjoyed school; she always made good grades and her teachers liked her. But Miranda has always been careful to keep her life balanced equally between work and play. "I get pretty good grades but I'm not the bookworm type. I'm more laid back. I'll do my homework at 10 o'clock and finish it at 1 in the morning. Once I had a teacher who really liked me but I don't think I was the teacher's pet. I think she just liked me," Miranda told *Cinema Confidential*. Miranda had fun at school, but she also enjoyed hobbies outside of the classroom, like horseback riding, piano lessons, and singing.

It was during elementary school that Miranda discovered another hobby that is still very important to her today—her love of movies. Miranda would spend hours after school glued to the television watching classic old films and new releases, which was probably why she didn't start her homework until so late most nights! As she watched the plots unfold on the screen, Miranda dreamed of being an actress someday. She would spend lots of time practicing lines from famous films in front of her mirror. She even used to convince her friends to reenact her favorite film scenes when they got together to play! Going to see movies at the theater was, and still is, one of Miranda's favorite things to do with her parents and friends on the weekends. Miranda loved to sing and dance, and watching all of those movies fueled her already creative imagination, so performing seemed like a natural next step for her. Little did Miranda know back then that her dreams of being a famous performer were going to take her much further than she had ever imagined.

Chapter 2

Big Discovery

When Miranda was only three years old, something happened that would change her life forever. Miranda's parents had planned a nice evening out together at Taste, a cozy restaurant on Los Angeles's famed Melrose Avenue. Patrons flock to Taste for its rustic Italian menu with modern American touches and intimate atmosphere. Fortunately for Miranda and her fans, Bill and Chris couldn't get a babysitter that night, so they brought little Miranda to dinner with them. Her parents may have been hoping for a night alone, but Miranda certainly didn't mind tagging along. She loved going out with her parents, especially to beautiful restaurants full of interesting people.

After ordering dinner, Miranda became bored with

the grown-up conversation. Deciding she needed to do something to entertain herself, Miranda slipped out of her seat and began to sing and dance quietly next to the table. She was having a wonderful time making up new dance moves and putting her own spin on her favorite songs. But as she performed, she began to sing louder and louder, oblivious to the fact that she might be disturbing other diners. Soon her performance had the attention of all of the nearby tables. Miranda's mom quickly shushed her daughter and got her to sit back down to eat dinner, but a talent agent dining a few tables over had already seen all she needed to see. The agent took a break from her own meal and approached the Cosgroves, asking if they had ever thought about getting Miranda involved in show business. The agent told Chris and Bill that she thought Miranda had real talent and wanted to sign her to her talent agency. "An agent asked [my parents] if I wanted to join her modeling and commercial agency. Of course, my mom went home and thought about it for a while, because she had never really thought about me getting into entertainment," Miranda explained to *Entertainment Weekly*.

Miranda's parents did have some serious reservations about involving their little girl in the entertainment industry. Hollywood isn't always known for being kind to its stars, and not every child can handle the kind of pressure it takes to succeed in the industry. Miranda would probably have to go on tons of auditions and get rejected from most of them before booking a single job. Chris just wasn't sure she was willing to put her daughter through that kind of rejection. Plus, Miranda would have to miss school and opportunities to spend time with her friends doing normal childhood things, like going to birthday parties, playing sports, and spending days at the pool, to go on auditions. Chris wanted her daughter to have a happy, carefree childhood and she was worried that allowing Miranda to go into acting and modeling would jeopardize that. But, despite all of her concerns, Chris knew that Miranda was talented and that she was happiest performing in front of an audience—the bigger the better! Plus, Miranda thought it sounded like fun. She had always been fascinated by movies and she begged her parents to at least let her try. She hadn't yet discovered that acting was her passion, but she was definitely intrigued by the idea. The Cosgroves finally gave in, and Chris took Miranda down to the agent's office and signed her up.

Miranda's new agent wasted no time sending the talented little girl out on as many auditions for print work and commercials as possible. Miranda was a natural. Even if she didn't have the right look for a job, she still aced every audition and impressed casting agents with her professionalism and poise. "I've actually always lived in L.A. which is a good place for auditioning if you want to be an actor, so I was lucky there. But actually, I hadn't ever really thought of being an actor, but when I was three, an agent walked up to my mom and asked if I wanted to do modeling and print. You know, you hear about that all the time, agents coming up to kids. Anyway, I just kind of did commercials and modeling and stuff, and I thought it'd be fun, and then when I was seven I really realized that I loved doing it, and that's when I started trying out for more theatrical things and actually roles and plays and stuff like that," Miranda told online magazine *Star Scoop*. Once Miranda got used to auditioning, she booked jobs easily and was completely at ease with her new lifestyle. Her parents really hadn't needed to worry. Miranda was completely unfazed by her successes and her failures. She loved booking jobs and was excited when she did, but she also understood at a very young age that being rejected was just a part of the business and she never took it personally. She remained the same sunny, energetic little girl she had always been and she really looked forward to auditions.

One of the first jobs that Miranda booked was a commercial for Mello Yello, a popular citrus-flavored soft drink. The Mello Yello ad was shot on a beach close to Miranda's home and it seemed more like an outing than work for the four-year-old. "I remember doing a Mello Yello commercial when I was 4 and thinking it was fun," Miranda told *Variety*. The Mello Yello ad was just the first of many for Miranda. With her big brown eyes, impish grin, and short dark hair, she was perfect for commercials and print ads. She did commercials for Burger King and McDonald's, as well as numerous catalog and clothing ads. It was fun for Miranda to do advertisements. She got to eat delicious fast food and hang out and play, wearing cool outfits. She also got the chance to meet other child actors and make new friends, all while doing something she loved.

As Miranda got older, she began to audition for larger roles. To prepare herself, she enrolled in acting classes at Warner Loughlin Studios. Warner Loughlin is a professional actress and performer who has worked in L.A. and New York in her many years in the entertainment industry. She's done it all—commercials, films, plays, and modeling—and eventually she started her own studio in 1996 to teach the tools of the trade to other performers. Her studio is extremely well-respected in Hollywood and she has coached hundreds of actors and actresses, including entertainment heavyweights like Amy Adams and Ryan Reynolds. Miranda and her mother felt right at home at Warner's and Miranda learned some valuable techniques there. Warner's famous technique teaches actors how to create genuine emotion in the moment of performing a scene instead of just reenacting emotion that the actor felt previously. The results are undeniably powerful performances, and Miranda was very lucky to have studied with such a great coach. "Warner's studio is such a warm and comfortable place. As a mother it's very important to feel [you're] bringing your child somewhere safe," Chris said in a statement on Warnerloughlin.com. Working with Warner and the other child actors in her classes helped Miranda blossom as an actress. She began to be more ambitious in the roles she went after, preferring bigger projects that challenged her skills to commercials and small ads. "I always feel confident and ready for my auditions having worked with Warner," Miranda explained on Warnerloughlin.com.

All of the preparation began paying off when Miranda was eight years old. "It wasn't until I was, like, 8, that I did much theatrical stuff," Miranda explained to *Entertainment Weekly*. Her first television role was a part playing the younger version of Lana Lang, Superman's love interest, on *Smallville* in 2001. Next she provided the voice for several characters in *What's New, Scooby-Doo?* in 2002, a modern revival of the popular cartoon from the 1960s. Miranda had always enjoyed watching the original *Scooby-Doo* cartoons, so getting to work on a few of the new episodes was really fun for her. She landed another animated role, providing the voice of Sarah in the episode "Morpholomew" on the Disney Channel cartoon *Lilo & Stitch*. Miranda must have been pretty excited to get to work on the show, especially since it was a spin-off of *Lilo & Stitch*, the movie, which was very popular when Miranda was little. She went on to land a guest-starring role on the hilarious sitcom, *Grounded for Life*, in 2004. Miranda played the part of Jessica, Lily's "little sister" in a Big Sister/Little Sister program in the episode "You Better You Bet." In the Big Sister/Little Sister program, Lily, a high-school girl, acts as a friend and mentor to Jessica, a girl in elementary school. Lily is a selfish and horrible "big sister" and Jessica gets fed up. Lily doesn't mentor Jessica at all; instead she makes Jessica do her hair, her nails, and listen to her talk endlessly about her own problems. Eventually Jessica tells Lily that her family is moving to North Carolina, but then Lily catches Jessica hanging out with a new big sister and causes a big scene! Miranda played the part perfectly. She was cute, spunky, and totally believable as the little girl that got the best of Lily, and she was a hit on the set. It was an invaluable opportunity for Miranda to learn the ins and outs of a sitcom and she made the most of it by paying close attention to the way the set was run.

As Miranda's reputation within the industry grew she became more and more in demand for roles, but Miranda was picky about what she chose to work on. "Well, my agency just sends me scripts of, you know, movies with good girl parts for my age, and I usually just go through them. Sometimes my parents go through them first, to like, check them out, and make sure they're okay for me to read. I just read through them and the ones I really like are the ones I go for the most," Miranda explained to *Star Scoop*. Miranda and her parents were always careful to make sure that Miranda didn't take on anything that would make her uncomfortable or that was too racy for a girl her age. The Cosgroves wanted Miranda to have as normal a childhood as a child actress possibly could. Miranda loved acting and performing, but if she had changed her mind about working at any point, her parents would have wanted her to quit. They only wanted her to perform as long as it made her happy. It really helped Miranda stay grounded to have such supportive parents who only wanted what was best for her. And with her career getting bigger and bigger, she would need all of the support she could get.

Chapter 3

Rock On

In 2002, Miranda auditioned for a hilarious movie written specifically for comedic actor Jack Black. Jack is a well-known Hollywood star with lots of movies under his belt, including *Shallow Hal*, *High Fidelity*, *The Cable Guy*, *Mars Attacks!*, *Saving Silverman*, and many more. The new movie was going to feature lots of child actors and there were several fairly significant parts for children. Miranda landed the biggest part for a child in the film, and she was incredibly proud of herself. "I was just so excited, but I have to say to prepare I went over the lines a little with my Mom and Dad and got to know what was going on. And I got really excited about meeting Jack Black, so of course I was really overwhelmed by that . . ." Miranda said in an audio interview with David

Stratton. Miranda was right to be excited. The comedy was called *School of Rock* and it would go on to be an incredibly successful movie, raking in big bucks at the box office and propelling Miranda to stardom.

School of Rock is about a singer and guitarist in his late twenties named Dewey Finn, played by Jack Black, who refuses to grow up. He sleeps all day, plays with his band at night, and never makes enough money to cover his rent or bills. When his band, No Vacancy, kicks him out of the group for his arrogance and crazy stage antics right before the big Battle of the Bands competition, Dewey vows to start a new band and win the competition himself. At the same time, Dewey's roommate, Ned Schneebly, a substitute teacher and former rocker himself, threatens to kick Dewey out if he can't come up with his rent money. Dewey is frantically trying to figure out how to pay his rent when he intercepts a call for Ned to substitute for a few weeks at a fancy private prep school. Dewey pretends to be Ned and takes the job teaching a class of fifth graders. Dewey does as little as possible, usually just allowing the kids to have recess all day, until he realizes that some of the kids are actually talented musicians. Inspired, Dewey decides to turn the class into a band and enter them into the Battle of the Bands. He puts the kids through auditions and sets them up as a band with backup singers, a crew, a costume designer, and even a manager—Summer Hathaway. Dewey teaches the kids valuable lessons about self-confidence and finding their own voices while educating them on music, the history of rock and roll, and showmanship, all the while hiding what they are really doing from the school principal, the other teachers, and the students' parents.

Once the band is ready, Dewey takes them on a field trip to audition for Battle of the Bands and secures them a spot in the show by pretending the kids are all terminally ill. Then, right before the Battle of the Bands, at parent-teacher night at school, Ned appears and Dewey is revealed for who he really is. He is fired from the teaching job and is ready to give up on his dreams. Luckily, the kids haven't given up on Dewey! They pick him up at his apartment on the way to the Battle of the Bands and help him realize that his real success has been helping them. They perform a special song written by the guitarist, Zack Mooneyham, in the competition and blow the crowd away—which includes their parents and the school principal, played by Joan Cusack, who have tracked them down when they go missing from class. The kids lose the contest to Dewey's old band, but they don't care. Their parents are actually very proud of them, they finally have self-confidence, and they've discovered how to follow their passions. Dewey himself has found a new passion—teaching. He and his roommate Ned decide to start an after-school program teaching rock music to kids.

Miranda played the part of Summer Hathaway. Summer is the class Goody Two-shoes and one of the few students without any musical talent. She even has a huge scene where she auditions to be a backup singer and belts out a horrible rendition of the song "Memories." After being assigned a position as a groupie, Summer rebels, so Dewey comes up with a special job for her: band manager. Ambitious Summer takes to her new role right away and starts studying up on the music business. She takes her position seriously and does a lot to help the newly formed band stay organized. Playing a teacher's-pet type was fun for Miranda. She is so naturally laid-back and easygoing that it was really funny for her to get to pretend to be the opposite when the cameras were rolling.

Miranda was the youngest of all the children on set, but she was also the most experienced, and her part was one of the largest in the film. Most of the other children were not professional actors. The casting agent for the film auditioned hundreds of children and cast them based almost solely on their ability to play musical instruments. To make sure that filming went smoothly, Richard Linklater, the film's director, held special rehearsals for the kids until they worked together like a real band. "We had like six weeks of rehearsals, too, before we started shooting, which is crazy. All I've ever done is have like one or two read-throughs at the most for a movie, and all of my rehearsals would be alone, at my hotel room. So this was definitely Richard Linklater's style to rehearse a lot, get it going like a well-oiled machine and then once we started shooting, all the songs were tight, except for some of my stuff," Jack Black told IGN.com. Jim O'Rourke, a professional musician, worked as the musical consultant on the film and he held a rock-and-roll boot camp for the band before rehearsals even started to make sure that the kids sounded like a real band by the time they started working with Jack Black.

Since the role of Summer was a larger one that required serious acting chops, the casting agent knew that they needed a pro. Miranda was a perfect fit. In addition to acting classes, Miranda had also been taking voice and piano lessons since she was little, so music came easily for her. But none of that would help her for her role as Summer. For *School of Rock*, she needed to sing badly. So Miranda worked closely with Jim O'Rourke to create a truly horrendous singing voice for her character. "He's [Jim O'Rourke's] really cool actually. There's one scene in the movie where Summer is supposed to sing bad. I'm actually pretty good because I've been taking lessons for five years. I got to have a 45-minute lesson with him on how to sing bad," Miranda explained to *Cinema Confidential*. Turns out that making her beautiful voice come out that badly was more of a challenge than Miranda had expected, and they had to do a few takes before Miranda even got close to sounding bad enough. "It's like kinda weird because the director would say, 'Now Miranda, try to even sing worse.' So, it was strange to hear him say that. It was really cool," Miranda said in an audio interview with David Stratton for *School of Rock*. But Miranda got it just right eventually, and that scene is one of the funniest in the entire film.

School of Rock is a hilarious movie, but it was even more hilarious working on the film behind the scenes. Miranda got the chance to work with lots of other kids her age and they had a blast together on set. Joey Gaydos Jr., Kevin Clark, Rebecca Brown, and Robert Tsai played the actual band members in the movie. Everyone first met at Jim O'Rourke's rock-and-roll boot camp and, since Miranda got her "bad singing" lessons during that camp, too, it gave her a chance to become friends with her castmates before filming. So once they did get on set, Miranda and her new friends had lots of fun goofing around. She and Rebecca Brown became especially close, and the girls still talk to each other on the phone about once a week. With that many kids on set, it wasn't always easy to keep order, especially if one of the kids got the giggles. "I mean, Robert? He had a little bit more trouble than the rest of us on that. And it was funny because when the camera went in front of him he'd laugh and that'd make us all laugh. So, it was a lot of fun," Miranda explained in an audio interview with David Stratton.

It wasn't all fun and games on set, though. The kids had to go to school while filming, too, as Miranda explained in an audio interview with David Stratton. "Well we actually have a studio teacher named Missy Sims but it's cool because you get a little bit of two sides, like actual school and we get to do like traveling to all sorts of different places and we practically had a different school room like every month, so its really cool, we get to get both sides." Much of the movie was filmed in New York, and it was definitely educational for a West Coast girl like Miranda to get the chance to see a little bit of the Big Apple.

Miranda also had a great time working with Jack Black. Jack is one of the funniest actors in Hollywood and Miranda probably learned a lot about comedic timing while doing scenes with him. And Jack certainly wasn't afraid to unleash his inner child while filming with the kids. "Yeah I'd always thought he was just so funny and I was really excited to get to meet him because I just knew he was gonna, of course, be funny, but he was a lot different than I had expected. He was like, a lot more laid-back . . . but he's just always, never stops twenty-four hours a day making us laugh. Yeah, it's really cool getting to meet him and work with him," Miranda said in a *School of Rock* audio interview with David Stratton. Jack loved working with the kids and he was easily the one goofing off the most during breaks. "In between scenes, we were just sort of compatriots. We were all in a platoon, on a mission. We were like peers, you know? They were rocking as hard as I was. And we would just hang out and fart around, and try to just stay loose. And that's one of the hardest things about making a movie is staying relaxed, because when you're waiting for the next scene that you're going to shoot, if you think about it too much, it can creep into your muscles, it can make you tight, and a bad actor. So, we tried to keep it loose," Jack Black told IGN.com. Jack gave the kids lots of funny nicknames, like calling Rebecca Brown "Reeba Deeba," and he became known for his improvisation skills. In the scene where Dewey and Summer are talking to the Battle of the Bands director, Jack picked up a chair and threw it across the stage during one take. Miranda had no clue he was planning to do anything violent like that and she jumped in surprise, but stayed in character and delivered the rest of her lines flawlessly. It looked so good that they used that take in the film. The final scene of the movie was also almost entirely improvisation led by Jack. It features Jack as Dewey and all of the kids rocking out to the song "It's a Long Way to the Top (If You Wanna Rock 'n' Roll)" at Dewey's new after-school rock program. Jack and the kids made up their own fun lyrics, like when Martha sings, "The movie is over, but we're still on screen," during her solo, and Dewey tells the audience that "It's time to go now . . . the people gotta come in for the next show!"

One of the biggest perks of working on *School of Rock* for Miranda was the exposure to new music she got on set. She was even inspired to take up a pretty rockin' instrument after filming. "Yeah, I learned a lot about music, yeah, like before I always liked the Beatles and Rolling Stones and basic, big rockers, now I'm getting more into, like, Led Zeppelin, and the Who, the Ramones, all those people, so I'm kinda more opened up to rock now and um, I'm playing electric guitar . . ."

Miranda said in a *School of Rock* audio interview with David Stratton. Miranda wasn't actually all that surprised that she really got into the music from the movie, especially since her mom had always been a fan of rock and roll. "My mom was always kind of into rock. After the movie, I went home and got out all her old albums and listened to them," Miranda told *Cinema Confidential*. And she wasn't the only one—it seems that most of the actors from the movie really got schooled in rock while hanging out with Jack Black. Miranda is even a fan of Jack's real-life band, Tenacious D.

The *School of Rock* premiere was Miranda's first big Hollywood premiere and she was very excited about it. She got to wear a cute, sleeveless, maroon dress and strut her stuff down the cheetah-print "red" carpet in Los Angeles. She posed for pictures with Jack Black and her fellow castmates, and got to enjoy the movie with a live audience. It was a very cool experience and it was Miranda's first real taste of stardom. She also got to attend a special showing of the film at the Toronto Film Festival—

it was only her first movie and Miranda was already an international sensation! Not bad for a ten-year-old!

Chapter 4

Drake and Josh

Around the time that *School of Rock* premiered, Miranda received some very exciting news. A pilot for a new show she had shot for the children's television network Nickelodeon was going to be picked up. Miranda was thrilled. The show was called *Drake & Josh* and it was written for teen comedians Drake Bell and Josh Peck, two former stars of *The Amanda Show*. Miranda's role was that of Drake and Josh's bratty little sister Megan. On *Drake & Josh*, Drake and Megan's mom marries Josh's dad and the two boys become friends despite their differences. Drake's character, Drake Parker, is a cool teen party animal who loves rock and roll and Josh's character, Josh Nichols, is a little bit of a dork who is smart and very well-behaved. Josh is thrilled to have a new, very cool stepbrother, but it takes Drake a while to warm up to Josh. Eventually the two become friends and they constantly get themselves into hilarious messes.

Miranda's character, Megan Parker, is Drake's younger sister and Josh's new stepsister. The show's creator, Dan Schneider, wanted Megan to be very different from the other younger brothers and sisters on television. Most of the time, younger siblings in sitcoms are bratty, jealous, and often whiny. Those characters typically follow their brothers and sisters around and are almost always tattletales who live to get their older siblings in trouble. The character of Megan was anything but a whiny tattletale. Instead, she was a devious, manipulative, creative genius with a talent for torturing and tricking her older brothers. Megan was also a master prankster, and her pranks became more and more extreme with each season of the show. "I get to do a bunch of pranks and I am always doing evil things to Drake and Josh," Miranda explained to *Starry Constellation*. Miranda was the perfect actress for the role—after all, she'd already proved she had plenty of spunk, attitude, and edge when she played Summer in *School of Rock*. With Miranda in the part, Megan quickly became one of the most popular characters on the show. "I think a lot of little girls like seeing me torture them [Drake and Josh]," Miranda said to msnbc.com.

The best part about playing Megan was all of the tricks Miranda got to play on her onscreen brothers. "I do a really amazing one where I make them [Drake and Josh] fall through the garage. They fall through their rooms to the garage. In the past, I've done a bunch of things like thrown tomatoes at them," Miranda told *Starry Constellation* excitedly. Of course, it's not quite as much fun to play tricks on people who are expecting the pranks and play along, but it was still cool to watch the boys handle the physical comedy required to pull the pranks off.

Megan's original tricks were fairly simple, but as the show progressed, so did Megan's ingenuity. In one episode she even ordered a live sheep off the Internet and blamed it on her brothers! By the last season of the show, Megan had advanced to using very high-tech gadgets to get her brothers in trouble. She had a whole wall of spy equipment in her room, including video surveillance, microphones, and recording devices. Megan may give her brothers a hard time on the show, but she also clearly loves them. In fact, when anyone else tries to pick on Drake or Josh, Megan is the first to defend them.

Miranda really enjoyed playing Megan. In real life, Miranda is one of the sweetest girls ever, so playing someone so mean was really fun. Miranda also got to grow up with her character on television. Over the course of five seasons, Megan and Miranda both went from being little girls to teenagers. Megan's storylines became more interesting as she grew older as well. By her last season, Megan was wearing cuter clothes and makeup, and she was dating and dealing with much more mature issues in school, with boys, and with friendships. Portraying Megan as she grew up really helped stretch Miranda's acting skills since she got to deal with all Megan's emotional changes as she became a teenager.

When Miranda joined the cast of *Drake & Josh*, she was only ten years old and she was very excited for the opportunity to work with Drake Bell and Josh Peck. She was already a huge fan of the boys and she was thrilled that she would be able to get to know them. "When I first auditioned for the show, I knew who they were because I had seen them [Drake Bell and Josh Peck] on *The Amanda Show*. I was so excited about the audition because I loved *The Amanda Show*. I had always thought they seemed really cool. When I got to the last callback, I got to meet Josh since I got to read with him. I thought, *I have to get this part!* He was just so cool when I met him and he's really funny. When I got it, I was just so excited!" Miranda told *Starry Constellation*.

The boys, however, weren't as excited right away to have a little-sister type on set. "We were walking to the writers' room, and I remember hearing the pitter-patter of these little feet behind me," Drake explained to the

New York Times. "She was just standing there saying: 'So where are we going? What are we doing?'" Drake and Josh were probably worried that Miranda would be annoying and not very fun to hang out with since she was so much younger than they were. But the boys quickly realized that Miranda was a lot of fun to have around and, once she got over being starstruck, she quickly became friends with her new costars. "Of course when I first started, I was really nervous about meeting Drake and Josh just from seeing them on *The Amanda Show*. I was like, so nervous about acting with them. I was like, Oh my God. But now it's really comfortable, and it's really fun," Miranda told *Star Scoop*.

Having to do silly or embarrassing things for her role in front of two cute older guys was probably a little hard for Miranda at first. After all, no one wants to look bad in front of cute boys! But Drake and Josh both made Miranda feel very comfortable, and soon Miranda stopped seeing them as cute boys and only saw them as her two goofy older-brother-like friends. And it was definitely fun for only-child Miranda to finally have some siblings, even if it was just on television! After working together for a few seasons, Drake and Josh became like real brothers to Miranda—and to each other. "They're [Drake and Josh are] very charismatic and they get along great with each other," Miranda told msnbc.com.

Miranda definitely looked up to the two boys. "They [Drake Bell and Josh Peck] are really cool. Drake is really awesome! He's really into the 80s and vintage things. He likes to swing dance. You can't be around Josh because you'll be laughing so hard that your stomach hurts," Miranda gushed to *Starry Constellation*. "Every single day has a memorable moment working with those guys. Drake taught me how to swing dance, which was really fun. I kind of want to keep doing it." Drake was already an established musician and he taught Miranda a lot about different types of music and helped her as she learned to play guitar. "It's just been so much fun getting to work with Drake and Josh. I mean, they're like two of the funniest guys ever, and they make me laugh every day a million times. So that's just been really fun. Drake's all into music and dancing, so it's been cool to get to like, be influenced by the music he likes," Miranda told *Star Scoop*. Josh was always there to listen if Miranda needed someone to talk to and he really encouraged her to find her own voice as an actress. And, of course, both boys made themselves available if Miranda needed to go over lines, rehearse, or if she needed acting advice for a particularly tricky scene.

Rehearsals often left Miranda, Drake, Josh, and the rest of the cast in fits of giggles. The funny actors were quick to jump in with an ad-libbed joke if someone flubbed a line or missed their cues—and some of the mistakes that happened on set were way funnier than anything that any of them could have made up. "We're constantly laughing. People mess up their lines all the time, but it's just funny. It's like a big family now, because, once you get to know everybody so well . . . nothing is embarrassing anymore.

So that's nice," Miranda told *Star Scoop*.

The *Drake & Josh* set was always a fun place to be. It was work and so they always got a lot done, but it was also a fun, relaxed environment that brought out the best in Miranda and her castmates. There was none of the cattiness or scandals that sometimes happen on sets. The cast and crew even hung out together after-hours! "We have a Friday night movie thing, everybody from *Drake & Josh* meets and we go see a movie every Friday night," Miranda explained to *Star Scoop*.

That family vibe definitely helped carry the cast through hard times, like when Drake was involved in a very serious car accident in December 2005. His 1966 Ford Mustang was completely totaled, and, unfortunately, there were no airbags to protect Drake. His face smashed into the wood-and-metal steering wheel and it fractured his neck, broke his jaw, knocked some of his teeth out, and left cuts on his face and chin. Drake had to undergo multiple surgeries to fix all of the damage, and he still has a few scars from the accident.

The cast was very supportive while Drake recuperated, sending him gifts and hanging out at the hospital to keep him company. Miranda was frightened by what happened to Drake, but it made her more thankful than ever for everything she had and more determined to make the most of all of the blessings in her life. Her goofy jokes and chill companionship were probably very comforting to Drake while he was getting better, and Miranda was always happy to spend the afternoon cheering him up!

Nickelodeon has a reputation for being a great place to work as a child actor, since the kids are stars and the entire company is geared toward that. "Kids who are in a movie, like Lindsay Lohan and others, are the only kids in a world of adults," Paula Kaplan, Nickelodeon Networks' head of talent, explained to *Entertainment Weekly*. "While our stars are at Nickelodeon, it's a world of kids. They spend all day long with each other and with their parents. They're able to build a strong structure with this security blanket around them, so they're well prepared when the real world hits." Miranda was really part of a family at Nickelodeon and they made sure she was happy, healthy, and well cared for when she was on set. Miranda's mom, Chris, came to the set every day and hung out with the other parents while Miranda was working so that she would be there if her daughter needed her for anything. Miranda was only legally allowed to work for five hours a day until she turned fifteen, so her shooting schedules were built around that time constraint with lots of time for her to do her school-work with a tutor. The director always gave the kids plenty of time for breaks, and there was a basketball court and break room with games where the kids could hang out between takes. Nickelodeon even puts all of its stars through an entertainment-industry boot camp called Talent 101 that teaches new stars like Miranda all about working on a television show. She learned what all the crew members do, how to handle interviews, and other invaluable information.

Miranda worked on *Drake & Josh* for four of the show's five seasons, but unfortunately she was filming a new Nickelodeon show during *Drake & Josh*'s fifth season and she couldn't do both. Miranda also appeared in the two *Drake & Josh* made-for-television movies. The first, *Drake & Josh Go Hollywood*, premiered in 2006 and the second, *Drake & Josh: Really Big Shrimp*, first aired August 3, 2007. In *Drake & Josh Go Hollywood*, Drake and Josh are supposed to take Megan to the airport and make sure she gets on a flight to Denver, but the boys get her flight number mixed up and send her to Los Angeles instead. Resourceful Megan makes the best of the goof-up and uses her parents' credit card to take a limousine to a swanky hotel where she books the presidential suite. Meanwhile, Drake and Josh hear a news report that a currency-printing machine has been stolen from an armored truck. It's around that time that they realize they put Megan on the wrong flight. The boys rush back to the airport and book tickets on the next flight to L.A. to go find her. On the flight Josh's G-O, a fictional MP3 player, gets switched with another person's G-O, but it turns out to be the G-O of the criminal who stole the currency-printing machine and the software he needs to print money is saved on that G-O. But Josh doesn't realize he has the wrong G-O until it's too late.

In the bathroom at the Los Angeles airport, Josh overhears a man saying he needs a musical act for an L.A. taping of MTV's *TRL* and he convinces him to book Drake's band. Excited, the boys go to Megan's hotel suite and the three of them try to pick a song for Drake to perform. This is when they discover that Josh has the wrong G-O and that the criminal and his friend have followed them. The boys manage to avoid the criminals by stealing Tony Hawk's red Dodge Viper sports car, which is parked outside with the keys in it. After a high-speed chase, the criminals manage to capture Drake and Josh. Everything looks hopeless until Megan shows up and confuses the criminals until the police arrive (after grabbing a little bit of counterfeit money for herself!). She heads off to Denver as originally planned, and Drake and Josh make it to *TRL* just minutes before showtime. The performance goes off without a hitch and Drake is invited to New York City to meet with Alan Krimm, a representative for Spin City Records, to discuss a record deal.

Miranda had a pretty large role in *Drake & Josh Go Hollywood*, and her fans were definitely thrilled that she had so much screen time. She was in lots of fun scenes—like riding around Los Angeles in a limo, partying in a posh hotel room, and foiling the criminals. Plus Megan got to be the one to really save the day in the end, giving her bragging rights over her brothers forever! Miranda's role in the second *Drake & Josh* movie wasn't quite as significant, but it was still a lot of fun.

Most of Miranda's scenes in *Drake & Josh: Really Big Shrimp* were shot on the regular *Drake & Josh* set, and they played up her comedic timing. *Really Big Shrimp* was filmed toward the end of Miranda's time on *Drake & Josh*, and they even make an allusion in the movie to the fact that Miranda will be moving on to star in her own show, *iCarly*. When the outside of the Premiere Theatre is shown, the movie listing on the marquee says "Now She's

Carly," which let fans know that Miranda was changing from Megan Parker to Carly Shay after *Drake & Josh*.

Drake & Josh: Really Big Shrimp picks up basically where the first movie left off. It opens with Drake performing his new song "Makes Me Happy" outside of the Premiere Theatre for Alan Krimm from Spin City Records. Alan loves the song and offers Drake a record deal. When the boys go to Spin City Headquarters to sign the deal, they get some great news—"Makes Me Happy" is going to be used in a tennis shoe commercial shown during the Super Bowl. Drake jumps into the recording studio while Josh handles the paperwork, but Josh is distracted by the large shrimp offered on the snack table. He ends up signing away the creative rights to Josh's song without even reading the contract! Alan Krimm has the song completely changed into, as Drake says, "horrible bubble gum pop garbage-y badness." Drake fires Josh as his manager, and to try to fix things, Josh switches the bad version of Drake's song with the original version so that the original version ends up in the commercial during the Super Bowl instead. Spin Records is furious and threatens to sue the boys and have them arrested, but the song turns out to be a hit. Nick Matteo, the president of Spin City Records, apologizes to Drake, fires Alan Krimm, and gives Drake a multi-record recording contract.

Meanwhile, Helen, Josh's boss at the Premiere Theatre, is getting married, and her grandmother Lula is staying at the Parker-Nichols home. Megan has to share Drake and Josh's room so that Lula can sleep in hers. Megan is not pleased about sharing with her brothers, so she redecorates their entire room with girly touches, feminine details, and potpourri. The only space she leaves Drake and Josh is a corner with an air mattress for two, a lamp, and a football. During the actual wedding, the Premiere Theatre accidentally catches on fire, but Josh manages to save the day and convince everyone to go on with the wedding as planned. Drake forgives Josh and re-hires him as his manager. After the wedding, Megan invites her friends over to help her move back into her own room. When Drake and Josh arrive, she tells them that

Nick Matteo sent over a ton of giant shrimp, but that she and her friends ate all but one of them. The movie ends with Drake and Josh fighting over the shrimp and then accidentally dropping it out the window, which is a direct reference to their very first scene together on *The Amanda Show*, where they fought over a shrimp on the ground.

Shooting made-for-television movies was a lot more involved that shooting a single episode of the show. Most regular episodes were shot entirely on a sound-stage at Nickelodeon Studios, but for the movies a lot of scenes were shot on location at the beach, in New York City, and all over Los Angeles. It was more like filming a real movie than a television show. Luckily, Miranda already had plenty of experience with that, so it was her turn to give advice to her castmates! Fans loved the *Drake & Josh* movies and Miranda loved working on them. But, after working on *Drake & Josh* for four years, Miranda was ready for a new challenge and Nickelodeon was ready to give it to her!

Chapter 5

Silver-Screen Star

While Miranda was working on *Drake & Josh*, she kept a pretty regular schedule. It was a little like being in school. She filmed for part of the year and then she had a few months off for vacation between seasons. It was nice to have a little time off, but Miranda loves acting and she couldn't sit around doing nothing for months at a time. So, to fill up that downtime, Miranda took on some roles in feature films.

One of the first movies Miranda did after *School of Rock* was an animated film called *Here Comes Peter Cottontail: The Movie*. Miranda had done voice-over work before in a few episodes of the television cartoon *What's New, Scooby-Doo?*, so she was excited to have the chance to work in animation again. This time she played the role of Munch, a baby mouse who loves to eat. In the movie, Munch has to help Junior, Peter Cottontail's son, and a bird named Flutter, save Easter. Irontail, an evil rabbit who wanted to be the Easter Bunny but didn't get the job, joins forces with the Queen of Winter, Jackie Frost, in a devious plot to make it winter permanently. The three unlikely heroes must go on a long journey to recover the stolen "Spring of Spring" to set everything right again. They eventually save the day, and become the best of friends in the process. Miranda had a lot of fun recording her role alongside her costars, Molly Shannon, Christopher Lloyd, fellow Nickelodeon star Keenan Thompson, and Roger Moore. It was a sweet film with amazing computer animation and catchy music, and the voice-overs Miranda did sounded great. *Here Comes Peter Cottontail* was never released into theaters, but it was released on DVD and is a favorite of kids everywhere, especially around Easter!

The next film Miranda worked on was especially cool since she got to film with Drake Bell, playing—

what else—brother and sister! The movie was a remake of the 1968 classic film *Yours, Mine & Ours*, which was based on the true story of the Beardsley family. In the original film, Helen North, a widowed nurse played by comedic actress extraordinaire Lucille Ball, meets and falls in love with Frank Beardsley, a widower in the navy played by Henry Fonda. The two date for a while before revealing to each other that they both have big secrets—Helen has eight children and Frank has ten! They fight their attraction, but they eventually get married and combine their two families to form one big family of eighteen kids! The new family moves into a big, rundown Victorian house. Can you imagine trying to share two bathrooms with seventeen brothers and sisters? The kids have a hard time adjusting to one another, but eventually they come together when Helen has another baby boy, making them a family of twenty-one! The writers made good use of Lucille Ball's comedic expertise, giving her plenty of physical comedy bits that really stole the show. The original film was nominated for a Golden Globe award for the Best Musical or Comedy of 1968. Miranda has always been an old movie fan and Lucille Ball is one of the most famous comedic actresses of any decade, so doing the remake of one of her films was something Miranda was very passionate about.

The 2005 version of *Yours, Mine & Ours* starred Dennis Quaid and Renee Russo as Frank and Helen Beardsley, and there were some definite changes from the original. Helen has ten kids and Frank has eight, instead of the other way around, and all of the children's names were changed. And instead of meeting randomly, Helen North and Frank Beardsley are high-school sweethearts who remeet when Helen moves back to town. They get married on a whim after reconnecting at a high-school reunion weekend, and only tell their children after the wedding has occurred. That's a pretty big surprise for their kids! The whole family then moves into an old lighthouse and tries to adjust to living together. The remake plays up the conflict between the two families by making Helen's character an artistic designer with very free-spirited children, while Frank is an admiral in the coast guard with a very regimented and disciplined family. "We're all so different, I mean on our side of the family. Rene Russo is like really free and she lets us do whatever we want and then the admiral's like really weird to come into our life because we have to follow all his rules and he has charts and [it's] just so much different," Miranda told RopeofSilicon.com. The oldest children in the film, Phoebe and Dylan North and William and Christina Beardsley, can't stand one another, but they decide to lead the other kids to work together to try to split up their parents. Their inventive plans eventually work, driving a wedge between Helen and Frank, who begin to contemplate getting a divorce. But by then the kids have come to like one another and they regret meddling. They help their parents get back together and the movie ends with the North-Beardsleys as one big, happy family. "We kind of make a plan to break them up together and I think that's probably the part in the movie where we all really start to like each other, because we have to come together to break them up. And that's when we realize that having a big family's really great," Miranda explained to RopeofSilicon.com.

Miranda's role was that of Joni North, the fifth-oldest child in the North family. Her character plays the saxophone and is very musical. "My character's name is Joni North and I'm kind of like the rooster in the family because I have to wake everybody up every morning with my saxophone. I've never played saxophone before, this is my first time. I got to take a couple of lessons, and it was so much fun," Miranda explained to Scholastic.com. Drake Bell played Miranda's older brother, Dylan North. His character was also very artistic and musical and he had one of the larger roles in the film as one of the oldest children.

It was great for Miranda and Drake to work together outside of *Drake & Josh*—after all, they already had the brother-sister chemistry down pat! But it was also really exciting for Miranda to get to work with so many other kids. "I'm really lucky to get to work with Drake again.

I did the *Drake & Josh* show with him. I made friends with a lot of people like Haley Ramm, who's playing Kelly in the movie," Miranda told Scholastic.com. Miranda and her new friends had a lot of fun goofing off between takes, playing games, and running around the Disney Ranch, where the movie was filmed. The lighthouse was real and it had plenty of space for the kids to hang out. "There's never a dull moment. It's so much fun on set. I'm an only child so it's fun. I'm having a blast on set with everybody," Miranda told Scholastic.com.

In addition to goofing off together during their down-time between scenes, the kids also had a lot of fun during the actual filming. The movie featured a lot of physical comedy, so Miranda and her castmates got to participate in some pretty amazing stunts, like a huge paint fight between the two families. "We have to do reshoots on the paint scene today. We did it last week, and it was so insane. We got to throw cake batter, which was supposed to be putty. Everyone was eating the cake batter.

We had pudding and all sorts of stuff that was supposed to be paint and glue. It was in our hair, and we had to go to school like that. We took showers here afterward. Hair and makeup helped us," Miranda explained to Scholastic.com. Having cake batter thrown at her was probably much more fun and probably tasted much better than real paint! Miranda did have a little bit of an advantage in that scene, since she had been in a food fight when she was younger. "[I was in a real food fight] in elementary school once, and it was a lot of fun. A friend of mine started it, and he had to clean up the cafeteria. He said it was worth it though," she explained to Scholastic.com. *Yours, Mine & Ours* was definitely one of the craziest sets Miranda had ever worked on, but that's what made it so much fun!

Miranda signed on to do another movie in 2006 called *Keeping Up with the Steins*. It was a smaller, less publicized film than *Yours, Mine & Ours* and *School of Rock*, but it featured some very big stars, including Garry Marshall, Jeremy Piven, Jami Gertz, Daryl Hannah, and

MiRANDA MaNia

Miranda shines on the red carpet.

Miranda with the cast of *Drake & Josh* at the Nickelodeon Kids' Choice Awards.

Miranda with Jack Black and her *School of Rock* castmates.

Miranda looking cute!

Miranda and the cast of iCarly with the show's creator Dan Schneider.

Miranda makes an appearance on MTV's TRL.

Miranda and her mom at an event.

Doris Roberts. *Keeping Up with the Steins* is the story of a young Jewish boy, Benjamin Fiedler, played by new actor Daryl Sabara, the thirteen-year-old son of Adam and Joanne Fiedler, played by Jeremy Piven and Jami Gertz, who is preparing for his bar mitzvah. A bar mitzvah is a ceremony that Jewish boys go through when they turn thirteen, and it marks their transition into manhood. Many Jewish girls go through the same process as they enter womanhood, but it is called a bat mitzvah. It's a very important moment in the Jewish faith and there is a lot of pressure on teenagers as they go through the bar mitzvah process. After attending the elaborate bar mitzvah party for the son of Arnie Stein, Adam's business rival, Benjamin's parents go overboard with their own party-planning. They rent out Dodger Stadium, hire Neil Diamond to sing, and invite big-name celebrities. However, Benjamin isn't even sure he wants to have a bar mitzvah, as he doesn't understand what it all really means and he has crippling stage fright.

To try and distract his parents, Ben secretly invites his estranged grandfather, Irwin, played by Garry Marshall, to come early. When Irwin arrives, everything changes. Irwin had a falling out with Benjamin's dad years before when he left Adam's mother. Because of Adam's own humiliating bar mitzvah, the anger Adam has toward his father clouds his judgment. Irwin causes a lot of problems, but he also solves a few. He really steps in and helps Benjamin understand what his bar mitzvah is all about and what it means to become a man. With Irwin's help, Benjamin gains the confidence to tell his parents that he doesn't want an elaborate party, but rather a casual get-together that celebrates the Jewish traditions he's so proud to be a part of. Even Irwin and Adam manage to reach an understanding and get along for Benjamin's sake.

Miranda played Karen Sussman, one of the girls in Benjamin's bar mitzvah class. The class is supposed to prepare kids for the ceremony so that they can perform flawlessly on the big day. Miranda's character is the class goody-goody. She is nerdy and claims to be a "late bloomer." She is always prepared for class and she tries to bond with Benjamin over the fact that they are not as cool as the other kids. Zach Stein, the boy whose bar mitzvah Benjamin's parents are trying to top, who happens to be one of Ben's best friends, gives Karen a particularly hard time. By the end of the film, Karen undergoes a big physical transformation. She ditches her glasses and ponytail, puts on a cute dress and some light makeup, and turns heads at Benjamin's bar mitzvah party. Zach is especially thrilled with Karen's makeover and it's clear by the end of the film that he has a thing for her. Miranda wasn't in many of the scenes, but she definitely stole the show when she was on camera. She was witty, confident, and dead-on as a slightly nerdy thirteen-year-old girl. Shooting *Keeping Up with the Steins* was a lot of fun, especially since all of Miranda's scenes were shot with the other kids in the film. Miranda also learned a lot about the Jewish faith while working on the film, which was very interesting for her since she has a lot of friends who are Jewish. It definitely gave her a new appreciation for what they go through during bar and bat mitzvah time!

Miranda shot her most recent film later in 2006. It's called *The Wild Stallion* and it's the story of two friends who discover a wild mustang. Miranda played Hanna Mills, a young girl who visits a ranch in the summer. There she meets C.J., played by Danielle Chuchran, a girl her age. The two girls become friends and band together to save the mustang when they uncover an illegal plot that puts the horse in danger. "I play a girl that comes from the city and goes to a ranch for the summer. She meets another girl that lives on the ranch and they end up finding a wild mustang. The girls end up taming it. It was a really fun movie to do!" Miranda told *Starry Constellation*. The film had lots of action sequences, adventure, and cool stunts.

Unfortunately, the movie was never released into theaters and went straight to DVD. It was one of the coolest sets Miranda has ever worked on and she did a lot of the stunts herself. She has been riding horses for years, so she was completely comfortable with all of riding she had to do in the film. "I had actually been riding horses for a while at that point. I don't think they knew I'd been riding horses, but I ended up doing it and it was really fun. We did it in Utah and it was really pretty there. We got to race and do all this cool stuff," Miranda explained to Scholastic.com. Miranda got along well with Danielle and the two girls are still friends. Working that closely with someone on such an adventurous set has a way of bringing people together. The two girls both loved riding and enjoyed giggling together about boys, clothes, and music. Miranda was a little disappointed that the movie didn't release into theaters, as she was very proud of her performance, but that happens often in show business, so she didn't let it get her down for long. In fact, shortly after filming *The Wild Stallion*, Miranda got some exciting news that would keep her very busy for a long time to come—she was getting her own show on Nickelodeon!

Chapter 6

iCarly

After her success on *Drake & Josh*, Nickelodeon was eager to capitalize on Miranda's talent and popularity. Dan Schneider, the mastermind behind *Drake & Josh*, *Zoey 101*, and *Unfabulous*, created a new show specifically for Miranda called *iCarly*. Miranda stars as Carly Shay, a young teenage girl who creates a web show with her two best friends. Carly is very laid-back and funny. She's the cool, girl-next-door type living in a modern downtown Seattle apartment. Carly's parents are in the navy and her older brother, Spencer, an eccentric and goofy sculptor, is her legal guardian. Sam Puckett is Carly's web show cohost and best friend. Sam is a wisecracking tomboy with a little bit of a rebellious streak and is definitely the "bad girl" in the friendship. Freddie

Benson is the *iCarly* technical producer and Carly's neighbor. He's slightly dorky and he's had a crush on Carly for years. The three friends have great chemistry, but it's really Carly who holds them together. Sam and Freddie bicker constantly, with Sam never missing an opportunity to insult Freddie or give him a hard time.

The web show acts as a show within a show during each episode, and fans can log on to a real website at iCarly.com where they can see clips from the fictional web show and post videos of themselves that could be chosen to appear on an episode of *iCarly*! *iCarly* was radically different than anything on television at the time and everyone was excited about the show's unusual hook, but they knew that wasn't enough—to really be a success, *iCarly* needed great characters and hilarious plotlines, and those just happen to be Dan Schneider's specialty.

Dan wanted to separate *iCarly* from *Drake & Josh*, and he worked hard to develop a character that was very different from Megan but was still spunky, interesting, and wouldn't alienate Miranda's fans who loved her as Megan. As Dan explained to the *St. Petersburg Times*, he was sure that Miranda could handle a drastically different type of character. "I was looking for someone to play it cool and be wise beyond her years. It's been real fun to watch Miranda hit that dead-on. Also, she's a beautiful girl, with amazing features—a doll to look at. Another thing, she's very classy. That's unusual in a little kid—the poise and the way she carries herself." But before Miranda could get into her character, Dan first had to get Carly just right. "Part of my job was to create a new world for her, a multifaceted character for her. I was a little concerned that kids and families who watch this would think this is just Megan pretending to be someone else. But I've checked the message boards and they don't see that; they see a new character," he continued. The transition from Megan to Carly was easy for Miranda, partially because she was working with a lot of the same people who she had worked with on *Drake*

& *Josh*. "I was in every episode, and worked with [*Drake & Josh* creator] Dan Schneider before he created *iCarly*. I think that helped a lot because I know him so well. It's nice to work with somebody you're really comfortable with," Miranda explained to *Entertainment Weekly*.

Miranda was definitely up for the challenge of giving her new role a unique and special voice! "Megan was really fun. She was always mischievous and I got to do crazy things with paintball shooters and stuff. Carly's more of a normal person. Megan was so mischievous and evil! It was really fun to play Megan. But now I get to play more of a real person. Carly deals with real problems. I really like that about her," Miranda told Scholastic.com.

One of the best parts about switching to a new show on Nickelodeon was that Miranda got to grow into an exciting, more sophisticated role while still remaining part of the safe, comfortable Nickelodeon family. Miranda knew that she would never be asked to do anything racy or anything that she felt uncomfortable about while working on a Nickelodeon show. "I always know the scripts are going to be kid-friendly," Miranda explained to the *New York Daily News*. "Plus, all my friends watch Nickelodeon, so it's cool." That was very important to Miranda since she loves her young fans and always wants to make sure that they can relate to the roles she takes on. Miranda's favorite thing about her new show is that Carly is a much more normal character than devious mastermind Megan. "It's different playing a character who is embarrassed and has problems with boys," Miranda told the *St. Petersburg Times*. "Carly is more like a regular person." Megan was a particularly fearless character, and not every teenage girl is always that confident! Miranda and Carly are more similar than Miranda and Megan ever were, so it was easy for Miranda to relate to Carly, although there are a few key differences between them. "She's [Carly's] really collected and she knows what to do when a problem comes up. She's really into her family and friends, and I'm like that too. But I'm not that much like her because she always knows what to do when there's a problem and I go crazy when faced with a problem!" Miranda explained to Scholastic.com.

Differences aside, one thing that Miranda and her character both love is the Internet. "I think the best part about the show is that it's interactive. It's really the first show for teens that has a great reality element to it, but it's still scripted. I think the cool part for me is seeing all the kids' videos. Thousands have already been sent into the website! And the show just came out," Miranda gushed to *Entertainment Weekly* right after *iCarly*'s first episode premiered. Seeing her fans' video responses and comments on iCarly.com was very gratifying and inspirational to Miranda, and it helped her understand more why Carly is so into her web show. "I also make little videos with my friends all the time. She's [Carly's] kind of into that," Miranda told *Entertainment Weekly*. "I've never actually posted them online before. We kind of just sing along to songs and do dorky stuff and then we'll watch it. Maybe I will now." If Miranda doesn't post her videos online, she can always pass them to the *iCarly* writers as ideas for new material!

Each episode of *iCarly* contains at least one segment of Carly and Sam's fictional web show. "The web show can be bigger or smaller depending on the episode. Sometimes, it may only be not that big of a deal, and then other times, it makes up the entire show. It's been nice—they've been balancing it very well. In some episodes, it's mainly about my life and the people around me. There are definitely boy troubles, and she gets in fights with friends—pretty much all the stuff that normal teenagers deal with," Miranda explained to *Entertainment Weekly*. The fact that most of the episodes are based on problems common to all teenagers no matter where they live makes it easier for Miranda and her costars to understand where their characters are coming from. "Yah, a lot of the skits have happened to me—so it's even easier to act it out if you've been through it," Miranda continued to *Entertainment Weekly*. The writers on the show often get advice from the teen actors to make sure that each episode feels authentic. They want *iCarly* to be as true to life as a television show can be! "Sometimes writers will come up and ask questions about certain words to make sure that kids, you know, still say that. We always crack about it because they'll say 'wonderful' in sentences that maybe kids these days wouldn't say," Miranda told *Entertainment Weekly*.

Miranda's castmates got into their characters just as easily as Miranda did. Jennette McCurdy, who plays Sam, has amazing chemistry with Miranda. In fact, it's hard to believe that they haven't been best friends since they were little. "We [Miranda and her *iCarly* costars] became friends as soon as we first met each other. I feel like I've known them forever. We see movies and hang out together. It's really fun," Miranda told Scholastic.com. The two girls bonded quickly over their shared love of movies and, of course, boys. "There are definitely cute guys on the show, and Jennette and I, we're always talking about it and whispering like high school," Miranda said to the *New York Daily News*.

Nathan Kress, who plays Freddie, also slipped into an easy friendship with Miranda and Jennette. "Nathan has a crush on me on the show, but in real life we're like best friends," Miranda told the *New York Daily News*. Miranda and Nathan bonded early on when they had to perform in several slightly awkward scenes in which Freddie confesses his love to Carly. Now, those types of scenes are some of their favorites to shoot because they are so funny. "We always crack up about that because every week he has to do some insane thing where he has to say that he loves me," Miranda told Scholastic.com. "I haven't had anyone like Freddie following me around, confessing his undying love! I've never had that in real life." Well, if Miranda ever does meet someone like Freddie, she'll know exactly what to do after all of Carly's experiences on the show!

One of the oldest actors on the show is Jerry Trainor, who plays Carly's older brother, Spencer Shay. Jerry also worked on *Drake & Josh*, but he almost never had any scenes with Miranda on that show. He played a movie theater attendant at the theater where Josh worked, but his role as Spencer is vastly different. His character on *Drake & Josh* was a little insane, while Spencer is more creative and goofy. "I threw myself into this role. Once the writers saw I would embrace whatever they threw at me, it was almost like a challenge to them to see what they could do to break me," Jerry told SignOnSanDiego.com. Having an actor who's willing to do anything for a laugh makes the writers' jobs a lot easier. They always have Spencer building some sort of crazy sculpture or engaging in a hilarious stunt. In one episode he builds a ten-foot-tall coffee cup and goes swimming in it. In another he decides to make a plaster mold of himself and spends almost the whole episode with a giant ball of plaster on his head! But one of the funniest episodes is the one where Spencer climbs into a heating duct and gets stuck trying to rescue a baby chick that Carly hatched for her science class. "I'm not claustrophobic exactly, but I was in this enclosed box with my arms by my side, so even if I did freak out, there was no way to get out," Jerry told SignOnSanDiego.com. "It was very hot on the set, and when the chicks would get scared they would poop, and that smelled horrible. And the little chicks were right in my face. Like, right up my nose."

Miranda loves her new show, but she has missed working with her old costars Drake and Josh. Luckily, they keep in touch and Miranda sees them often. "Yeah. I talk to them [Drake Bell and Josh Peck] all the time. They've both visited the set. I think they were talking about directing an episode," Miranda told Scholastic.com. Fans would definitely love to see Drake and Josh make an appearance on *iCarly* and Miranda isn't counting that possibility out, as she continued to Scholastic.com, "That would be awesome. We were talking about having them [Drake Bell and Josh Peck] do a cameo or something. I don't know if it will end up happening. Drake walked into a scene one day. It was really funny. He just showed up and for fun, I was sup-posed to go to a door and open it and he was there. I was freaking out. I was really shocked." Miranda may be the star of her own show, but she'll always have a special bond with her on-screen brothers!

The cast of *iCarly* gives a little shout-out to *Drake & Josh* in the episode "iWanna Stay With Spencer." In that episode, Carly's grandfather says that he is going to stay at the "Parker-Nichols Hotel," referring to Drake Parker and Josh Nichols, Drake and Josh's fictional characters on *Drake & Josh*. And Drake and Josh aren't the only Nickelodeon stars that have gotten in on *iCarly*. References to *iCarly* have been written into several of Dan Schnieder's other shows on Nickelodeon, most notably *Zoey 101*. *Zoey 101* tells the story of a teen girl named Zoey and her roomates, Lola and Quinn, at a formerly all-boys boarding school. The girls often clash with their guy friends, Logan, Chase, Michael, and Dustin, in hilarious ways but they always make up in the end. In the episode "Anger Management," Lola logs on to iCarly.com and a video of Logan screaming at Dustin is posted on SplashFace.com, a fictional website from the *iCarly* episode "iPilot." In another episode of *Zoey 101*, Lola chooses a new ringtone for her cell phone that is a digital version of the *iCarly* theme song, "Leave It All to Me."

iCarly premiered on Nickelodeon on September 8, 2007 with "iPilot." Fans loved the show and immediately started visiting the fictional show's real website, uploading videos of themselves doing funny things for *iCarly*'s producers to consider for the show, and commenting on how cool they thought the show was. The *iCarly* website makes it easy for fans to upload videos using a special application on the site—just like Carly and Sam's fans do on the TV show! In the first episode, Carly gets blamed for one of Sam's jokes at school and the two girls' punishment is to judge the auditions for an upcoming talent show. They film the auditions and then load them onto the school's website, but what they don't realize is that the video they post also contains footage of them making fun of one of their teachers, Ms. Briggs. The teacher does not appreciate their teasing and she refuses to put any of Carly and Sam's picks into the talent show. Carly and Sam are really disappointed until their classmates weigh in and tell the girls how much they loved their commentary. That gives Carly and Sam the brilliant idea to host their own web show, and their friend Freddie volunteers to be their technical producer. For the first episode, the girls ask all of the talent show acts that they liked to guest star. The web show is a hit and they decide to do one every week.

Miranda was so excited that fans enjoyed the show, but it was a little overwhelming. Overnight, she became a bigger star than she had ever been before. Luckily, Miranda was prepared for it, having seen the kind of response that Drake and Josh always got from fans. "It made it comfortable because she got to see [Drake and Josh] go through it before she went through it," Miranda's mom, Chris Cosgrove, told *Entertainment Weekly*. "The pilot was fun because she was ready for it." The fan response to the pilot was more enthusiastic than even optimistic Miranda had expected. That kind of response would have made a lot of actresses arrogant, but those nearest and dearest to Miranda weren't about to let *iCarly*'s popularity go to her head! "I'm excited that the show has done so well and that kids are getting into it. It helped that I did *Drake & Josh*, because I got to watch them do it. So I know exactly what I'm getting into. I'm friends with all my friends from elementary school—they think it's cool that I'm in acting, but they don't think it's that big of a deal," Miranda told *Entertainment Weekly*. Dan Schneider certainly wasn't worried about his star turning into a diva. "She's a star," he said to the *New York Times*. "She is one of the classiest little girls that I've ever met. I don't believe I've ever heard her complain about anything, I don't think I've seen her in a bad mood once in my life, and I've done 61 episodes of television with her. I really avoid the overly trained Hollywood kids . . . Miranda's the real deal; there's nothing Hollywood about her." Miranda took all of the success in stride. She was too focused on her new character and delivering the best performance she possibly could for her fans to worry too much about her rising star status.

Luckily, fans continued to tune into *iCarly* and the show got better and better with every episode. Upbeat rock band, the Plain White T's, gave a performance on one episode and the writers introduced funnier physical comedy gags and silly guest stars to keep the action fun and fresh. They even did an *iCarly* special that was broadcast live on iCarly.com called "*iCarly*: Live from Hollywood" to promote the 2008 Nickelodeon Kids' Choice Awards. In the special episode, Spencer is hired to make a Nickelodeon Kids' Choice award blimp out of cocktail wieners. He brings Carly, Sam, and Freddie with him to the Pauley Pavilion in Hollywood for the 2008 Kids' Choice Awards ceremony. Carly, Sam, Freddie, and Spencer explore the backstage area of the awards—going through the gift bags, sneaking into Jack Black's dressing room, and stealing mini-wienies from the snack table to finish the sculpture. In the end, Spencer's sculpture is destroyed by the snack table lady.

With the glowing reception that each episode and special receives from fans, *iCarly* is sure to be on the air for a long time to come—and Miranda couldn't be more excited about that. She wants to keep working on the show as long as it makes her fans happy, and her fans certainly can't wait to see how the show develops in the future!

Chapter 7

Sing it, Miranda

Miranda has always been very into music, although most of her fans didn't know that until recently. Miranda was discovered while singing in a restaurant at only three years old, after all, so it should be no surprise that Miranda can really belt it out. She's taken voice and piano lessons since she was five. And, while on the set of *School of Rock*, she was inspired by all of the amazing rock-and-roll music and decided to learn how to play the electric guitar. Unfortunately, *School of Rock* also had an unintentional negative effect on Miranda's musical career. For her role as Summer in the film, Miranda had to sing badly in a very memorable solo. It was a stretch for Miranda, who actually has a lovely singing voice. She was so bad at singing badly that the film's musical consultant had to give her a special one-on-one lesson to ensure that she sounded bad enough. It took several takes, but Miranda finally managed to belt out her solo so horribly that the director was blown away. It was perfect for the film, but after that most people thought that Miranda actually couldn't sing!

Despite the fact that most of her fans thought she was tone deaf, Miranda continued to take music lessons. She loves singing and playing musical instruments, especially her guitar—a very cool pink electric guitar with flowers on it. Kicking back and playing guitar is a great way for her to relax and unwind after a long day on set. Who knows, maybe someday soon she'll be writing her own hit songs! Miranda's favorite music to play is catchy, upbeat rock-and-roll and pop music. She learned a lot about the history of rock music from Jack Black and her mom has always been a big rock-and-roll fan, so Miranda grew up listening to bands like the Rolling Stones, Boston, the Police, and Journey, to name just a few. But Miranda doesn't limit her music to all old favorites. She also loves more modern music like the Plain White T's and Gwen Stefani. Gwen is one of Miranda's favorite singers of all time and she is really inspired by Gwen's fashionable style and the way she fuses pop, punk, and hip-hop in her music. Miranda even got the chance to introduce Gwen's music video "Early Winter" on her visit to MTV's video countdown show *TRL* on January 17, 2008. Miranda wore a cool purple satin dress with her hair up in a messy French twist and red lipstick (Gwen's favorite shade!). She hung out with hosts Lyndsey Rodrigues and Damien Fahey and helped them count down the top ten videos of the day as voted on by MTV viewers. Then she got to introduce a current video of her choice and Miranda's pick was "Early Winter." *TRL* is one of MTV's most popular shows and Miranda loves watching it, so it was a very cool experience for her to get to appear on the show and give a shout-out to one of her favorite artists!

Working with Drake Bell on *Drake & Josh* also really inspired Miranda musically. Drake is an amazing performer who has released two gold albums, *Telegraph* in 2005 and *It's Only Time* in 2006, and three popular singles. Drake plays the guitar and writes lots of songs, and his character on *Drake & Josh* was also a musician. Drake performed often on the show and he always had his guitar on set with him. Watching Drake write and play between takes and in his downtime while filming was motivational for Miranda. It was amazing to see someone who was so passionate about his music in action almost every single day. Drake loved that Miranda was into music, too, and he was always more than happy to help her when she was learning a new song or needed help with a tricky chord transition while learning to play guitar. And once she really had the hang of playing, the two would often have jam sessions on set.

Dan Schneider, the creator, executive producer, and writer of *Drake & Josh* and *iCarly* definitely took notice of the musical chemistry that Drake and Miranda had together. Dan had already written Drake's musical talent into *Drake & Josh*, and when he was creating *iCarly* he saw a golden opportunity to showcase Miranda's considerable abilities. So when Dan needed a theme song for *iCarly,* he asked Miranda to team up with Drake and record "Leave It All to Me." Drake cowrote the song with some other popular songwriters and Miranda loved it. It was the perfect optimistic, upbeat, spunky song to introduce fans to her new character, Carly Shay. So Miranda and Drake went into the Columbia Studios and recorded the song as a duet. It came out better than Miranda ever could have hoped and she was very proud of all of the hard work the two had put in. It was actually Miranda's first time in a recording studio to lay down tracks for a song. Drake's smooth tenor voice was a perfect complement to Miranda's enthusiastic alto and their two voices blended perfectly for a polished sound. Miranda had done voice-over work in the past for several animated projects, but singing on a recording was a different experience. It was also great for Miranda to get one last chance to work with Drake. She was excited about her new show, but she was also disappointed that she wouldn't get to see and hang out with Drake and Josh every day anymore.

When *iCarly* premiered on Nickelodeon, Miranda was excited for a number of reasons. It was her first television show as the big star and she wanted it to do well, but she was also psyched for fans to hear her singing the theme song. She was very pleased with the final result and so were her fans! As soon as the show aired, they began trying to find the song to download online. Columbia Records eventually released the song as a single at *iCarly* fans' requests and it made it to number 83 on the Billboard Pop 100 chart and it squeaked in at number 100 on the Billboard Hot 100 chart—not bad for a girl who didn't have a record deal or any publicity! The single was also released onto iTunes and Rhapsody, and Miranda fans have made it one of the most popular downloads on the Web. Since "Leave It All to Me" has been so well-received by fans, Miranda has her fingers crossed that Dan might write in some other opportunities for her to sing on *iCarly*. Since the show centers around Carly and Sam's webcast, it would be pretty easy for Carly to sing or play guitar on her show. Hopefully Miranda will be singing her way into season two!

Chapter 8

Guest Starring Miranda

Talented Miranda was becoming a bona fide movie star and super-celebrity, and people were sitting up and taking notice. People were very interested in her story, and she did interviews on lots of popular talk shows like *The Today Show*, *The View*, *Dr. Phil*, and *Good Morning America*—sometimes more than once! Miranda was also a frequent guest at award shows like the *MTV Movie Awards* and the *Nickelodeon Kids' Choice Awards*. She even swung by two of MTV's hottest shows, *Beat Seekers* and *TRL*. But Miranda's favorite appearances were the ones she made on Nickelodeon. She got to attend special Nick events, like the *All That: 10th Anniversary Reunion Special* hosted by Frankie Muniz, and she often hosted *Teen Nick*, a special block of programming for teenagers on Nickelodeon every Sunday night. When Nickelodeon wanted to promote Miranda's new show they dedicated an entire night of *Teen Nick* to Miranda. They called the night "Miranda Madness" and it aired on August 10, 2007. Miranda was featured as a special guest star in every show that night just for "Miranda Madness." The night kicked off with a classic *Drake & Josh* episode featuring Miranda in her familiar role as Megan Parker, but then things got even more interesting as Miranda took on a variety of new roles and characters.

The second show of the night was *Just Jordan*, a comedy about Jordan Lewis, a teen from Little Rock, Arkansas, who has just moved to Los Angeles. Jordan is a little bit of a fish out of water in California and the show focuses on the trouble he gets into as he tries to adjust to life in his new home. Jordan is a total basketball fanatic. Miranda played the role of his basketball coach's niece, Lindsey. Lindsey is an exceptionally sheltered piano prodigy. She loves piano, but she is miserable because she's never gotten the chance to be a normal kid. She doesn't know how to relate to other kids her age or how to kick back and have fun. When Lindsey meets Jordan they make a deal—she'll give him piano lessons if he will teach her how to be a regular kid. Jordan is in a bind and needs to learn some piano basics fast! Lindsey helps Jordan, and, as promised, he teaches her how to slack off once in a while and to enjoy music other than classical compositions for piano. But Jordan's lessons work a little too well. Lindsey likes being a regular kid so much that she decides to quit playing piano. Eventually, Jordan convinces her not to give up on her dream. Miranda loved guest starring on *Just Jordan*. Lil' JJ, the actor and stand-up comedian who plays Jordan is hilarious, and he was always cracking jokes between takes. And since it was only the first season of *Just Jordan*, it gave Miranda an opportunity to begin to get to know the relatively new cast.

Next, Miranda joined the kids at Pacific Coast

Academy when she guest starred as Paige Howard in an episode of *Zoey 101* titled "Paige at PCA." Paige is a science genius who is visiting PCA to test her latest invention there. She is a year younger than Quinn, PCA's resident science star, but she has already invented a revolutionary proton converter, which will boost the energy efficiency at PCA by twelve percent and is garnering tons of media attention. Quinn feels completely lost since she is no longer the school's top science student, and she begins skipping classes and slacking off. However, when Paige's proton converter malfunctions and Paige can't fix it, Quinn steps in and saves the day.

Zoey 101, starring Jamie Lynn Spears in the title role of Zoey Brooks, is one of Nickelodeon's most popular shows, and it was already in its third season when Miranda made her appearance. The cast got along really well and all of the actors are good friends, which made guest starring a blast. The kids welcomed Miranda with open arms, and Miranda loved getting out of the studio and filming on location at Pepperdine University, where all the show's outdoor scenes were shot. Miranda made friends with the *Zoey* actors and actresses and she keeps in touch with them regularly, so one of them may make an appearance on Miranda's show one of these days.

After her time at PCA, Miranda joined the cast of *Unfabulous* for the first episode of season three, "The Talent Show." *Unfabulous* is a show all about a quirky, creative middle-school student named Addie Singer who plays guitar, writes her own songs, and struggles with popularity and friendships at school. Miranda guest starred as Cosmina, school hottie Jake Behari's childhood friend. In the episode, Addie is determined to win first place in the talent show by teaching her dog Nancy to perform tricks. Jake Behari, Addie's boyfriend, is supposed to help her, but Cosmina puts a kink in Addie's plans. She asks Jake to perform an old magic act that they used to do in the talent show. Cosmina's boyfriend was going to do it with her, but he couldn't make the show at the last minute, and Jake is the only person who knows the routine well enough to fill in. Addie becomes jealous and insecure when she sees beautiful Cosmina and Jake together, and does everything she can to get Cosmina out of the picture. She manages to lock Cosmina in a closet right before showtime. Then Addie takes Cosmina's place in the magic act so that she can perform with Jake. But when Addie gets onstage, she finds Cosmina's boyfriend there instead of Jake! He hadn't been any happier than Addie at the thought of Cosmina performing with Jake and managed to make it to the show. In the end, Addie's friend Gina wins the prize with Addie's original act and Addie learns that jealousy does not pay!

Unfabulous was Miranda's favorite show to guest star on since she happens to be very good friends with Emma Roberts, the actress who plays Addie. It was a relatively small role for Miranda, but it gave Emma and Miranda a chance to hang out on set—plus Miranda got to do some fun, flirtatious scenes with

Raja Fenske, the supercute actor that plays Jake Behari! Miranda and Emma have both been acting for a long time and they became friends after running into each other at audition after audition when they were younger. The girls have tons in common—they've both been in lots of movies, play guitar, sing, and love vintage clothes! Miranda would definitely love to work with Emma again in the future, so who knows, maybe there will be a Miranda and Emma movie sometime soon if they have anything to say about it!

Miranda doesn't always get guest-starring roles handed to her. For "Miranda Madness," roles were written into each show specifically for Miranda, but most of the time she has to audition, just like everyone else. But it can work to her advantage if the casting directors are familiar with her previous work. "... sometimes when I try out for auditions, of course, I've found that a lot of the casting [directors'] kids or people who ... work there, [their] kids will know the show [*Drake & Josh*], which is kind of cool," Miranda told *Star Scoop*.

Miranda would love to do more guest-starring roles, if she could ever find the time! It's much easier for her to fit in movie roles, since most shows tape at the same time and she's usually too busy filming her own show to take a week off for a guest spot. "Miranda Madness" was such a cool experience for that very reason—Miranda got to guest star in not one, but three shows! It was a wonderful excuse for Miranda to get to know lots of her fellow Nickelodeon stars better and to show off her versatility as an actress. Whether she was playing a devious little sister, piano prodigy, science genius, or beautiful magician, Miranda stole the show with every part. But the real purpose of "Miranda Madness" was to prepare Miranda fans for her newest project—her very own show on Nickelodeon. They showed sneak-peek clips of the new show throughout the night, which left fans curious and excited for the upcoming premiere of the show that would propel Miranda to superstardom—*iCarly*.

Chapter 9

Off Camera

Miranda's career is really taking off. With all of the work she's doing, it's amazing that she ever has any time off! But when Miranda isn't on location shooting a movie or on the *iCarly* set, she's just like any other fifteen-year-old girl. She lives in Los Angeles with her parents and has an adorable poodle named Pearl. It took a while for Miranda to convince her parents to let her have a dog, as she told GratedCheddar.com in November 2005. "I'm hoping for a big ol' puppy for Christmas, I've been begging for one and I already found the puppy I want, so I'm hoping for that." So Miranda was incredibly excited when she got Pearl for Christmas that year. She had a lot of fun training her new puppy and now Pearl is a very important part of the

Cosgrove family. Miranda loves Christmas, especially when she gets gifts like a puppy, but her favorite holiday is Thanksgiving. "I just love Thanksgiving, you know being with your family and everybody coming over and getting to see everyone and all the good food," Miranda explained to GratedCheddar.com. Holidays are always special for Miranda because it's guaranteed time off to hang out with her parents.

Miranda is homeschooled because of her hectic schedule, so when she does get a few weeks off, she doesn't have to spend it in the classroom, and she tries to make the most of that time. But even time off can't always compare to doing what she loves best—acting! "Sometimes I get kind of bored if I go like a month or so and I'm not doing anything. At first I'm like, 'Cool, I'll have a little time off and I'll get to hang out with friends,' but then after a little while goes by I'm like, 'Oh,' and I really wish that I could go back and start doing work again. It's just a blast to get to come in to the set and say hi to everyone and work with the people you know.

After a few months it seems like everybody's like family," Miranda told the *New York Times*. Miranda might miss working and all of her friends on set when she's away, but having time off does have its advantages. She gets to indulge in her hobbies, spend time with her non-actor friends, and catch up on her schoolwork. "I did regular schooling up to 5th grade and then started homeschooling. I have a tutor on set and I do school four hours on rehearsal days. We rehearse three days and shoot two. And the two days that we shoot, we only have to do an hour of school, so we have more time to film and stuff, and we get an hour lunch break," Miranda told *Entertainment Weekly*.

When she's not on set, Miranda sticks to a more regular school schedule. She completes her classes in the mornings and then has afternoons free. "I actually do online school. It's my first year doing it, it's really strange. Last year I did homeschooling more, now it's like an online thing . . . The program I'm with actually has a day where you go and you get to meet kids and like, take classes, which is really cool. So I've gotten to do that, which is fun. You get to meet new people, and kids your age," Miranda told *Star Scoop*. When Miranda does get the chance to make new friends outside of the entertainment world, it's always a real treat for her. It's also cool for her to compare notes about her classes with other students doing the same work. There are times when Miranda does miss going to a regular high school with all of her old friends, but she does get to go to "fake" high school on the set of her show and, as Miranda explained to the *New York Daily News,* "All my friends are in high school, so they're keeping me close. I don't miss out on anything."

When Miranda isn't doing schoolwork, she can often be found pursuing one of her favorite hobbies, as she explained to *Star Scoop*. "I actually, as far as sports go, I actually fence, and I horseback ride, and I play the guitar, which is really fun." Miranda got into horseback riding several years ago and she loves the rush she gets from galloping down an open trail with the wind in her hair.

"Oh, actually my friend lives in Burbank, and I go to the Burbank Equestrian Center. She went all the time, and I thought it was really cool, and I was always jealous, because, who didn't love horses? So one day she actually asked me to go with her, so I went, and I've been taking lessons, and doing it ever since," Miranda told *Star Scoop*. Miranda got the chance to put those horseback-riding skills to good use in her role in the movie *The Wild Stallion*. She got to do a lot of stunts herself because she was so good on horseback, and it was really fun for Miranda to work with horses all day on the job. After all, she usually only gets to ride on her days off! Taking a day off just to go riding and enjoy the beautiful, sunny California weather is the perfect way for Miranda to unwind and relax. But when Miranda wants to really work up a sweat during her downtime, she plays tennis or fences. "I got into fencing a while ago so sometimes I do that. It's really hard though. People think it's easy, like in *Pirates of the Caribbean*, but it's super hard.

The instructor that did a lot of stuff on *Pirates of the Caribbean* is actually at the fencing place I go to and he talks about it all the time," Miranda explained to Scholastic.com. Fencing is certainly a challenge, but Miranda enjoys taking on new activities that push her limits. Plus fencing is great exercise and keeps Miranda in top physical shape. And who knows, maybe someday Miranda will get to use her fencing skills for a role, too.

On top of all of her hobbies, Miranda also spends a lot of her time off just relaxing and hanging out with her friends. "Basically, I just hang out with my friends and go see movies constantly. I'm a movie junkie, I love movies," Miranda told *Star Scoop*. You'd think Miranda would get enough of the movies at work, but no, this girl watches more movies than most producers in Hollywood! She loves comedies, action films, romantic tearjerkers, and just about anything with Rachel McAdams or Orlando Bloom. Whether she's sitting in the dark in the plush, velvet seats of her local theater with a big tub of popcorn in one hand and a giant soda in the other, or curled up on her sofa watching a DVD in her pajamas, Miranda sees several movies every week. Luckily, one of Miranda's best friends and movie buddies just happens to live right next door to her, which is pretty convenient, as she explained to *Star Scoop*. "I hang out with my friends all the time, my next-door-neighbor is my age, and she's a crack up, and I hang out with her all the time . . . I've pretty much stayed in touch with all my friends from school, because I went to elementary school all the way through, so I'm friends with all of them. So we hang out all the time, see movies together." Miranda has some amazing friends who are also in the entertainment business, but her very best friends are the kids she grew up with at Maude Price Elementary School. They don't treat Miranda any differently than they did back on the playground in first grade, which is really nice for a star like Miranda. It helps keep her down to earth and it gives her a much-needed break from Hollywood to hang out with them, as Miranda explained to *Star Scoop*. "I'm lucky because all of my friends are from elementary school, so they just see me as the same dorky Miranda that they knew before. So they still think I'm a total dork, the TV show doesn't help. It's kind of nice sometimes when people recognize you and it's really cool, like, to be with your friends, and people come up to you." Miranda loves meeting her fans, and her friends think it's pretty cool that she makes so many kids laugh every day.

Miranda does make her fans laugh, and she also keeps her friends giggling. She's just as funny offscreen as she is on-screen, and she even has a few hidden talents. "I can shake my eyes. I have an extra eye muscle, so it looks like everything is shaking," Miranda told the *St. Petersburg Times*. But Miranda is a really good friend in a lot of other ways, too. She can always be counted on to keep her friends' secrets; she even has a special system to keep track of everything people have told her. "I do have a journal, that I write all my thoughts in every day. So that's kind of something. I also have a burn box where I write secrets down and put it in a box.

Like umm, secrets you've heard from people and stuff like that, I have them in a box in my room," Miranda explained to GratedCheddar.com. Once she writes a secret down, Miranda gets it out of her system and then she isn't tempted to repeat it to anyone.

To keep in touch with her friends when she's on set, Miranda likes to call or email during her breaks. Just like her character on *iCarly*, Miranda spends lots of time online! "Yeah, I'm on the Web a lot. I like to play games online. Sometimes I play *Sims*," Miranda told Scholastic.com. Miranda is also addicted to instant messenger, since it allows her to chat with her friends who are far away. "I'm sort of tech-savvy—I IM [instant message] my friends all the time and I'm always online," Miranda said to the *New York Daily News*.

Whether Miranda is keeping busy with hobbies, hanging out with friends, or just watching a good movie, she always knows how to make the most of her time off. And, working as hard as she does, Miranda definitely deserves the break. But we know she'll never take too much time off, because she loves acting way too much, which is very lucky for all of her fans!

Chapter 10

Miranda's Style

Miranda is known for her fresh, bold, girl-next-door style when it comes to fashion. Whether she's all dressed up for a red carpet appearance or just kicking back with her best friends for a trip to the mall or the movies, Miranda always stands out in a crowd. If you want to make Miranda's laid-back, California-cool look your own, here are some tips.

First, start with brights. Miranda loves bold colors and fun, graphic prints. Her favorite colors are red-oranges, maroons, turquoises, and the occasional touch of black to add a little sophistication. Even with a simple outfit, Miranda likes to add a punch of color, like a bag in a primary color or a pair of neon ballet flats. She also likes to wear hooded sweatshirts and jackets with fun, busy prints. Miranda is 5' 5", so she can definitely pull off big prints!

For premieres, industry parties, and award shows, Miranda sticks to sophisticated and classy dresses with feminine touches and unique details. She likes lace, ribbons, and satin fabrics in baby-doll cuts with short or three-quarter-length sleeves. She likes to pair dresses with dark tights and flats or low heels. She always keeps the rest of her glamorous look very simple. She will occasionally wear a simple pendant necklace, but otherwise she skips the jewelry altogether.

Most of the time, Miranda saves the glam look for special occasions. When she's hanging out at home, she favors jeans, cute T-shirts and tank tops with girly details, and sneakers. Her favorite sneakers are Converse high tops and Vans slip-ons. Her character on *iCarly* dresses a lot like Miranda does. The costume designers put Miranda in lots of dark-wash jeans with layered tops and jackets and sneakers. Carly and Miranda both have sporty vibes that are just a little bit on the feminine side. Some of the brands Carly wears on the show are Luxirie by LRG, Kimchi & Blue, and Free People. Luckily, Miranda likes the same brands, which comes in handy when she gets to keep some of her clothes from the show!

Miranda has one big weakness when it comes to shopping—she loves vintage clothes. She and her friends have lots of fun browsing through the funky vintage boutiques all over Los Angeles when Miranda has a day off. Miranda knows she'll always find something one-of-a-kind with a cool story behind it when she shops vintage. If you don't have any vintage shops near you, you can always raid your older sister's, aunt's, or mother's closets or head on over to your local Goodwill store. You'll be surprised at some of the adorable clothes you can find for great prices! And it's even easier to find great old jewelry and bags at shops like that.

No look would be complete without hair and makeup. Miranda doesn't wear much makeup when she's just hanging out and she lets her long hair air-dry most days. But when Miranda is on set, she gets made-up by professionals. To give her the fresh look she's famous for, Miranda's stylists blow dry her shiny dark hair and use hot rollers to give it a little bit of volume. They use barrettes and headbands to give her hair a polished, finished look. Then the makeup artists use a little blush, a few coats of mascara, and a neutral lip gloss. When she's dressing up, Miranda goes for the same basic look, but adds a little bit of eye shadow for a smoky effect, and a darker red lip gloss. Miranda likes to keep her makeup light, even on the red carpet, so that her natural beauty can shine through.

Whether you are mimicking Miranda's easy-going, California-casual vibe, her bold but feminine *iCarly* look, or her glamorous starlet evening style, make sure to wear your clothes with confidence and a big smile and you'll look just as great as Miranda!

Chapter 11

Future Plans

Miranda is truly a star on the rise. With two hit television shows, multiple movies, and a rockin' single under her belt, Miranda has already accomplished more in her first fifteen years than most people do in an entire lifetime—and she's just getting warmed up!

Luckily for Miranda's fans, Nickelodeon is solidly behind *iCarly* so there are sure to be many more seasons to come. They have already ordered forty episodes for season one and are sure to order just as many for future seasons. Miranda is certainly excited about the upcoming seasons of her show. Carly is very unlike any other character that Miranda has had the opportunity to play, and Miranda is enjoying pushing her acting skills and exploring new situations within the role. She is also psyched to get to keep working with Jennette McCurdy, Nathan Kress, and Jerry Trainor, since they all have such a great time filming together. *iCarly* made-for-television movie specials are definitely on the horizon and are sure to have cool, slightly over-the-top plots that will take Carly, Sam, and Freddie's web casts to the next level.

But that doesn't mean *iCarly* is the only project Miranda will be working on. She loves guest starring and will definitely be making some more appearances on other Nick shows. She's good friends with a lot of the other Nick actors including Drake Bell, Josh Peck, Emma Roberts of *Unfabulous*, and Devon Werkheiser from *Ned's Declassified School Survival Guide*, and many of them will probably get to make appearances on upcoming seasons of *iCarly*! Josh Peck is even scheduled to direct an episode of *iCarly* in season two.

In addition to television appearances, Miranda is sure to be gracing the silver screen again soon. She loves the diverse challenges movies offer, but Miranda is holding out for the right roles. She wants to find parts that allow her to stay true to herself and her fans, but also push her skills and allow her to grow as an actress. Miranda loves working on both movies and in television, and she's not willing to give up either one, as she explained to *Star Scoop*. "I actually like both. I mean, with movies, it's fun, because you get to travel [to] different places and stuff like that, and plus it doesn't take as long. But I love being on a TV show because you get to know the people so well, just from seeing them everyday. And, you get to come back, which is fun. It's not as sad either, at the end, because you know you have another season coming. So that's nice. It's very different. With movies, we usually have [a] single camera, and during the TV shows, it's much different with the four cameras, at least that's the way we shoot it. But, I like both ways. I don't know, I would love to do both."

Miranda is hoping to model her career after her favorite actresses. "I love Rachel McAdams—I think she's like the coolest person ever. All my friends love her, too. I love *The Notebook* and *Mean Girls*. And Reese

Witherspoon is really great," Miranda told *Entertainment Weekly*. Rachel McAdams and Reese Witherspoon are huge stars, and while they are most well-known as film actresses, they've also both had guest roles on popular television shows.

Miranda is certainly well on her way to achieving the kind of career that her role models have. She already has some of the coolest fans in the world, as she explained to GratedCheddar.com. "One fan asked me to sign their sock. That was crazy. They just took off their shoe and handed me their sock and asked if I'd sign it." With fans who love her that much, Miranda can count on them to support all of her future televisions shows and movies.

Miranda might be best known for her acting chops, but she is also very musical. She has signed an amazing record deal with powerhouse music label, Columbia Records. Miranda's first album will be part solo record, part *iCarly* soundtrack. It will include four of Miranda's original songs, including "Leave It All to Me," as well as popular songs by other hot artists. The album will be called *iCarly Playlist*. After its release Miranda will head back into the studio to record a second album—and this time it will be all Miranda. And since Miranda learned how to play the electric guitar after her role in *School of Rock,* maybe there will even be some rocking guitar solos! We can't wait!

With such a successful career, it's hard to imagine Miranda as anything but a performer, but Miranda is keeping her options open. "I definitely want to go to college. That's a big thing with me. I have a few friends that we're like already planning, and we want to go to the same college, which would be really fun," Miranda told *Star Scoop*. Hopefully, Miranda will get the chance to continue her entertainment career while pursuing higher education. Miranda may even end up in a college class with you someday—how cool would that be?

Talented, ambitious, and funny, Miranda already has all of the makings of a true superstar. With her career burning white-hot, we're sure to be seeing more and more of Miranda in the future—and we know that her fans can't wait to see what she does next!

Chapter 12

Fun, Fast Miranda Facts

So you think you're Miranda's biggest fan? You've seen every single episode of *iCarly* and *Drake & Josh*, you've downloaded "Leave It All to Me" on iTunes and know the words by heart, have *School of Rock, Yours, Mine & Ours,* and *Keeping Up with the Steins* on DVD, and have submitted numerous videos of you and your friends to iCarly.com. Well here are some of the basic fun facts that every true Miranda Cosgrove fan should know by heart!

Full Name: Miranda Taylor Cosgrove

Date of Birth: May 14, 1993

Parents: Bill and Chris Cosgrove

Siblings: None she's an only child

Hometown: Los Angeles, California

Eye color: Brown

Hair color: Dark brown and naturally straight

Height: 5' 5"

Nickname: Mirry Furry

Star sign: Taurus

Hobbies: Fencing, horseback riding, playing *Guitar Hero*

Instruments: Piano and guitar—a pink guitar with flowers on it

Favorite actor: Orlando Bloom

Favorite actress: Rachel McAdams

Favorite movie: *Love Actually*

Pets: A poodle named Pearl

Favorite pizza topping: Pepperoni

Favorite food: Pastries—especially danishes

Favorite clothing: Anything vintage

Celebrity crush: Justin Timberlake

Most prized possession: Her Sidekick phone

Favorite ice cream: Mint chocolate chip

Favorite TV show: *American Idol*

Favorite colors: Pink and green

If she wasn't an actress she'd like to be:
A marine biologist

Chapter 13

iMiranda

Miranda Cosgrove is one busy girl! Whether she's auditioning for a new movie, doing schoolwork, horseback riding, fencing, filming a new movie or her hit Nickelodeon show *iCarly*, or just hanging out with friends, there's no telling where she'll be next or what she'll be doing! So if you want to keep up with the spunky starlet, here is a list of websites with all of the latest Miranda information all the time!

You can do a lot of cool stuff on the Internet, like play games, chat with friends, or watch hilarious web shows like *iCarly*, but Miranda would always want you to be careful when you are hanging out online. Never give out any sort of personal information—like your name, address, phone number, or the name of your school or sports team—and never try to meet someone in person that you met online. And never surf the Web without your parents' permission.

When you are online, please remember that not everything you read there is true. There are lots of people creating websites, and sometimes they make up information to make their sites more exciting. Can't find your favorite website? Websites come and go, so don't worry—there's sure to be another Miranda site to replace it soon!

www.iCarly.com

This is the official *iCarly* website. It has clips from the show, games, blog entries from Carly, Sam, and Freddie, pictures, quizzes, and a place where you can upload a video of yourself doing something cool and funny. Some of the user-submitted videos even end up on the television show!

www.imdb.com/name/nm1388927

This is the Miranda Cosgrove's official Internet Movie Database page. It has photos, a biography, a filmography, and a detailed list of all of Miranda's television appearances.

www.miranda-cosgrove.net

This is a totally awesome Miranda fan site. It has pictures, links, wallpaper and icons, lots of news updates, and forums where you can chat about all things Miranda.